Granny's Gang

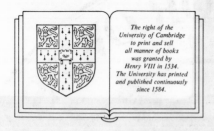

The right of the University of Cambridge to print and sell all manner of books was granted by Henry VIII in 1534. The University has printed and published continuously since 1584.

Published by the Press Syndicate of the University of Cambridge
The Pitt Building, Trumpington Street, Cambridge CB2 1RP
32 East 57th Street, New York, NY 10022, USA
10 Stamford Road, Oakleigh, Melbourne 3166, Australia

First published by Greey de Pencier Books, Canada 1984
© Greey de Pencier Books, 1984
This edition first published by
Cambridge University Press, 1987

Printed in Canada

ISBN 0 521 351715 hardcovers
ISBN 0 521 359694 paperback

A PLACE FOR OWLS

by Katherine McKeever

Illustrated by Olena Kassian

Cambridge University Press

New York   New Rochelle   Melbourne   Sydney

Contents

Chapter 1
A PLACE
FOR OWLS

It is almost dusk, and as I turn away from the window beside my desk, the last light of day reflects an orange glow from the eyes of a big owl sitting behind my chair. I lean back for a moment and blow softly into her neck feathers. She grunts contentedly and closes her eyes, as if to savour the moment. When I stop, the owl opens her eyes to see why. Then she nibbles gently at my hair and around my ears. This is Granny, a Spectacled Owl. Not knowing that she and I are different kinds of creatures, Granny thinks I am her mate.

Although Granny is very special to me and my husband Larry, she is only one of over a hundred owls of all sizes and types that share our lives. We operate a place called The Owl Rehabilitation Research Foundation in the Jordan Valley of Southern Ontario. Our windows overlook a wide river estuary bordered by cattail marshes and filled with water lilies. Our house is on a high bank covered with tall oak and hickory, ash and white pine. I lived in this valley years and years ago, when I was a little girl, and now I am happy to be back home again.

When we decided to move back to this valley, it wasn't just to sit and admire the scenery. Larry and I came back to work. Over the years we realized that something very worrisome was happening to wildlife, especially to the animals who control the numbers of other creatures below them in the food chain by preying upon them. These predators were rapidly disappearing.

The cause of the problem was people. People were cutting down the forests and ploughing the prairies and draining the swamps. The land was being bulldozed and covered with big shopping malls, houses and factories. Millions of animals were being killed every year along our highways by high-speed trucks and cars. These fast-moving killers are especially dangerous for night creatures such as foxes, raccoons and owls. Blinded by headlights, they don't see the big machines behind the terrible glare. As if all this wasn't bad enough, some irresponsible people were shooting, trapping and poisoning the predators as well.

Upset by the slaughter, Larry and I decided to try to help at least one kind of predator survive in a world of people. We decided on owls—or, to be more accurate, one small owl helped us decide on helping owls.

The owl responsible was a nestling Screech Owl that had been stolen from its parents and then turned over to our local Humane Society. There was nothing they could do to help it, so we persuaded them to let us try. We borrowed library books about raising wildlife, but there wasn't

much about owls. The books said that insects, worms and mice were good for Screech Owls. We scurried around trying to catch some mice and moths, without much success. The worms were easier—we had big dew-worms in our cherry orchard. But to our horror, the little owl sickened and died in just ten days.

When I gave the Screech Owl's little body to an ornithologist and asked what had happened, he told me that our big dew-worms were contaminated by the pesticides farmers spray on their fruit trees. I was broken-hearted to think I had accidentally killed our tiny owl with poisoned food.

This sad experience prompted Larry and me to begin to plan how we could use the rest of our lives to help wild owls. Gradually, as word of our interest in injured owls spread, the frightened victims of our urban world began to turn up at our door in odd-shaped boxes and baskets and even feed sacks. And, almost as frightened as our patients, we entered the world of veterinarians and their operating rooms and their instructions for home care and medication. We began to learn what rehabilitation was all about; saving some, losing some, seeing the quiet suffering and always being touched by the beauty and dignity of these wild creatures.

That was more than fifteen years ago, and we are still "up to our eyes" in owls. Over a hundred new arrivals come to us every year from all parts of Canada and the United States. They arrive by car and air express, and almost half of them will be rehabilitated. When they leave us, these owls have a good chance of surviving again in the wild. We always try to release them near their original homes, even if that means the other side of the continent.

Other owls never leave us. Although we can help them back to good health, they never regain full use of a damaged wing or eye. Some of these injured owls are the most important owls we have. They "mother" orphaned juveniles so that the young owls grow up normally and can be released back into the wild again. These injured "substitute parents" are the owls you'll read about in this book. Like Granny, many of them live with us and think they're part of the family.

Raising and rehabilitating hundreds of owls hasn't been easy. We have had to build more than fifty outdoor compounds, great big flight cages much larger than rooms in human houses. They contain pools and trees, stumps, special perches and nest boxes or platforms. There are only two or three owls in each compound, and we make sure they have lots of places to hide—from us and from each other, if they want to. Most of all, we have to give them the best food for owls, and that means *mice*! I never dreamed we'd need so many mice! When there are 125 owls staying here, we need about 250 mice every day! Because we could never catch that many ourselves, we drive hundreds of kilometres every week to pick them up from breeding laboratories. In case of emergencies, we keep a small colony of breeding mice ourselves. That way we always have a fresh mouse for a newly arrived baby owl or owl that's badly injured.

Finally, we have to raise a lot of money every year to buy the mice and build the cages, to pay for surgery, medications, air express from distant places and long distance telephone calls. Raising that much money, chauffeuring owls around and picking up mice takes most of Larry's time, although he tries to do a lot of other things too. Most of my time is spent cleaning. I clean the owl cages and the mouse basins and the house. And in the evening, if my cleaning is done and the owls are tended to, I work at my desk, keeping notes on all the owls' activities for that day.

So here I am, this lovely spring evening, with Granny watching over my shoulder as I write. I hope you will enjoy reading about the owls that have enriched our lives as much as we have enjoyed living with them. And while you are laughing at their antics, maybe even shedding a tear, I hope you will come to think of them as unique and beautiful creatures. Then, perhaps you could help other people to see them this way too.

Chapter 2
GRANNY
EARNS HER NAME

No other owl in North America looks like our Granny. She is bigger than a chicken and has a big black head, white eyebrows and whiskers and huge orange eyes. With her pumpkin-coloured breast feathers and black wings that fold around her like a witch's cloak, she is the perfect Hallowe'en owl. Her legs have fluffy, deep yellow feathers right down to her toes, and like most owls, she has very big feet. It's hard to imagine a place in nature where Granny's rich colours would fit right in, but she is a jungle owl from South America.

What is a Spectacled Owl like Granny doing in a place like Canada? Sometimes I wish we knew Granny's early story, but perhaps it's just as well we don't because the little we do know makes me very angry. Granny was brought to us by a friend who found her in a dirty little box in a small zoo where she'd been left by her previous owner several months before. She was thin and cold and wet, and I'm sure she was very sad and lonely. Looking at the pictures we took of her then, it is hard to believe she is the same beautiful owl that lives with us today.

Unlike most of the owls that arrive at our centre, Granny didn't have broken bones or damaged eyes, so with a lot of loving care she slowly returned to good health. But there was something wrong that we could never fix—Granny didn't know she was an owl. She was our first experience with an owl that had never seen its own parents. It takes baby owls about two weeks to focus their eyes well enough to see their mothers and fathers and get used to the way they look. Granny must have been taken from the nest so young that she never saw her own parents. Instead, when her eyes began to focus properly, she was among people. So she grew up thinking humans were her family and her species.

"Imprinting" is the name for what happens when young birds identify with the creatures they see most often. Granny was imprinted on people so she had no trouble accepting us as her friends. When she was an adult she even began to think of me as her mate.

In her early days with us, I would admire her lovely colours and sometimes feel sad knowing that she would never see her jungle home. I'm sure it must have been a beautiful place, with bright flowers and pools and little

14

birds on jewelled wings. But the important thing now was getting Granny back into good health and trying to give her the very best life we could. Along with gentleness and affection, this meant the right food and big cages. Her indoor cage—the size of a small bedroom—was built into a sunny downstairs level of our house. Her outside cage was almost twice as big. To keep her feet healthy, we brought branches and limbs of every type and thickness and dragged big stumps into her cages. We even gave her

a big nest box in each cage, just in case. She also had to have big pools filled with clean water. Even her indoor pool was big enough for her to spread out in because, like all owls, Granny loved to splash about. The newspapers on the floor around her pool were often soaked when she had her daily bath.

For the first two years that Granny lived with us we didn't know whether she was male or female because there's no way of telling the sexes apart just by looking at an owl. The amazing thing is that owls seem to know about each other right away. I wish I knew how. Perhaps they can tell by the pitch of the other owl's voice, but then again sometimes they don't say anything when they first meet. Maybe it's some expression in their eyes that I can't see or the way they can flatten some feathers and puff out others. Whatever their secret is, we just had to take a chance on Granny's name. We called her that because of the big white granny spectacles around her eyes. Luckily for us we had guessed correctly!

Two years went by, and Granny became part of our lives. Outdoors, she seemed to enjoy watching all the activity around her cage. She watched the little birds and chipmunks, squirrels and groundhogs, even the fish splashing out in the estuary. Indoors in the wintertime, she spent her evenings on her carpeted roost behind my desk chair. Sometimes she would fly off to investigate other parts of the house, but she was seldom gone for long and always returned with a swoosh to her perch near me. She was a completely delightful creature, gentle and affectionate with me, always so interested in what went on and more than a match for our dogs and cats with her silent, orange stare.

Then came December of her third year. She had come

inside the month before and was her usual playful and loving self. In fact she seemed even more loving and playful than usual. All day long she called to me from her downstairs cage, and in the evenings upstairs she would constantly nibble at my shoulders and hair. If I left the room even for a moment, she either followed me or croaked like a bullfrog until I returned. It seemed as if Granny was just crazy for attention, and no amount of grooming from me kept her quiet for long. It was all very odd and a little worrisome.

Then suddenly everything changed. Granny didn't want to come upstairs anymore. She didn't even want to be picked up. When I tried, she just flopped awkwardly back to her perch, grunting unhappily. More surprising still, she lost all interest in food, and Granny had been an owl who loved her daily mouse. Now the mice I brought her were left on the food ledge untouched. Even her eyes had lost their sparkle. There was definitely something very wrong with Granny, and we became increasingly worried about her. We took her temperature, but it was normal. We watched her every half hour or so, but all she did was sit dozing on her perch. Sometimes she would get into the unused nest box high in the corner of her cage and do her dozing there, in the gloom.

Although she had never paid any attention to the nest box before, she now seemed to be in it all the time. Sometimes she just sat quietly; other times she scratched around peevishly as if trying to get more comfortable. "What *is* the matter with you, Granny?" I asked one day as she sat there lumpishly, making grumpy little noises deep in her throat. I tried to comfort her, stroking her breast feathers and grooming around her face—all things she used to like—but she just made irritable little chittering

sounds and moved away from me. Now we were really frightened and wondered if she was dying. We thought of medicines, but without any evidence of disease there was no use trying them. I sat up all night with her that last night, hoping I could encourage her to stay alive. We had called the veterinarian, and he said he would come in the morning.

As I think back on that terrifying time, I find it hard to believe we were so stupid and unimaginative. There was nothing the matter with Granny at all. She had just been busy manufacturing her very first egg. And what a glorious egg it was too. Obviously anything that perfect must have taken a lot of concentration. Larry and I admired the egg. Granny admired her egg. And there was an air of relief and celebration all over the house. We thought of opening some champagne, but since Granny had done all the work, it seemed more appropriate to get her a nice fresh mouse. And just to make the day perfect, she ate the mouse in one gulp.

Chapter 3
GRANNY'S EGG

Now it's one thing for an owl to lay an egg, but it's quite another to produce an egg with a chick in it. Because Granny was the only Spectacled Owl we had, we knew that her egg had not been fertilized. But there was no use telling Granny that. She looked so smug and was such a model mother that it seemed an innocent game to pretend her egg would hatch.

Unlike the restless days before the egg arrived, Granny was now full of bustle and industry. She spent hours rearranging the soft pine needles and wood shavings we had put in her nest. She turned her egg carefully at regular intervals and instinctively knew that it was important to wet her breast feathers to keep the egg from drying out.

She called imperiously for her daily mouse and croaked indignantly if anyone but me came near her cage. Sometimes she would stand up and peer between her feet as if to make sure the egg was still there. Or was she simply admiring it? Now that she was much too busy with her egg to come upstairs in the evenings, I spent a lot more time downstairs with her. I had the feeling that she considered me not only her mate, but the father of her egg. As a "new father," I discovered responsibilities I hadn't ever thought of before.

Not only was I expected to supply Granny with fresh mice at regular intervals, but she insisted that I do guard duty too. I think she liked to see me outside the cage cooling my heels. If I tried to sneak away it wasn't long before I would hear her croaking anxiously for me to return. She made me realize how nervous a female bird on a nest can be, and how important it is to have a protector nearby, especially when she has to leave the nest for a few moments. Granny always let me know when it was time for her to bathe or defecate by making a special little urgent hooting sound.

Three weeks passed by in this busy routine, but in the fourth week there was a subtle change. Granny called for her daily mouse a little earlier than before, then a lot earlier. By the end of the week she wanted two mice every day. "She can't be getting hungrier," I said to myself, a little perplexed. "She's just been loafing around in her nest all month." But there was no denying that she was getting very impatient about her mice. The strange thing was that although she grabbed the mice from me very quickly, she didn't seem to be eating them. Filled with curiosity I fetched a stool so that I could climb up and peer into her nest box to see what she was doing with them all.

What a surprise! Neatly stacked in the corners of the nest box were the last three or four days' supply of mice. She hadn't been eating them at all–she'd been *storing* them. But for what? There could be only one answer–she was hoarding food for the baby she expected to hatch out of her egg. As if to confirm that I had guessed correctly, the next time I brought her a mouse she did an extraordinary thing. She grabbed the mouse, and standing on the edge of her nest with the mouse hanging from her beak, she dangled it over her egg and began to make soft, coaxing, food-offering sounds. I couldn't believe my eyes! Did she really expect the egg to reach up and grab the mouse?

We were fascinated to see that her instincts were stronger than the evidence of her eyes. I could see her egg, *she* could see her egg, and yet here she was offering food to it as though it were a chick. Then I reminded myself that Granny, like all wild creatures, has a "built-in clock" that triggers changes in her body and behaviour. This clock responds to increasing or decreasing hours of light and warmth.

I had brought Granny indoors in the late fall, and she was suddenly surrounded by warmth and light. And because we were close to each other again, I was able to groom her regularly and have her near me in the evenings. Is it any wonder, with all this warmth and attention, that her clock told her to get going on an egg? But what was to be done now? We couldn't bear to think that Granny's first experience with an egg would end in disappointment, and yet there was no way her egg was going to hatch. Obviously we had to find an egg that *would* hatch, and we had to find it fast. Granny was already geared up to being a mother.

Larry and I had a desperate talk. Where on earth could we find an owl's egg, any owl's egg, that was ready to hatch in January? Impossible. Well then, we wondered, what about a chicken's egg? If it hatched, Granny would find a baby chicken instead of an owl, but maybe she wouldn't notice the difference, at least not right away. Anyway, what was worse—no baby at all or the wrong kind of baby? There was only one way to find out...

Off we dashed to the chick hatchery a few miles away and convinced the owners we needed a big white egg that was due to hatch that very night. Fortunately, chicken eggs look just like Granny's, and we brought the precious egg home wrapped in cotton wool on a hot water bottle. Now how were we to put it under Granny and remove her own egg without her throwing a fit?

We decided to create a distraction so that I could make the switch. We thought a lively mouse would make a good decoy, since Granny hadn't seen one that could run

for quite a while. But we didn't quite bargain for what
happened. At the first squeak of the mouse, Granny was
out of her nest box with all her feathers standing on end.
Heaven knows what the mouse thought at the sight of her!
I set the mouse down on the floor of the cage, and for

just an instant they both stared at each other. The next
moment the mouse was streaking for its life, with Granny
right behind it. I had forgotten to close the cage door, and
out went both mouse and owl, right across the room.
There was a dreadful crash as the mouse reached cover
under a small table and Granny, all beak and talons, hit
the screen beside it. The screen went flying in one direction
and the mouse in another. Granny was too out of practice
to change direction that fast and grabbed at a lamp, which

went over too. In the noise and commotion I almost forgot to switch the eggs.

Meanwhile, breathless and looking a little sheepish, Granny gathered herself up off the floor. She gave a few indignant croaks and flounced back to her nest. I breathed a sigh of relief as I watched her step carefully around the new egg, apparently unaware of the difference. As for the mouse, we never saw it again. It might still be living with us somewhere.

All evening I kept creeping quietly downstairs to listen for anything that sounded like a baby. But all was silent. Nothing is so worrying as quiet when you are waiting for a certain sound. Midnight came and went and still no baby peeping. At one o'clock I peeked in again. Granny was dozing peacefully on the new egg. The same thing at two o'clock. Larry had gone to bed long since, muttering about the lateness of the hour, but I hovered on the stairs near Granny's cage. Finally, at three o'clock in the morning, I gave up and went to bed, but not to sleep. My ears strained for the sound of a chick peeping, far into the night.

Chapter 4
GRANNY'S CHICKEN

W e woke up the next morning to the loudest cheeping sounds in the world. The chick must be right under our bed, I thought as I sat up and looked around. At the very least it must have got out of Granny's cage and be squealing at the bottom of the stairs. I ran downstairs, my heart in my mouth, but there was the chick, safe in the nest. How could anything so small make so much noise? As for Granny, her eyes were bulging with excitement as she whirled around in her nest trying to keep her new baby under her breast feathers where it belonged. It was obvious that the fuzzy little yellow blob had good legs and a mind of its own.

As fast as Granny zipped after it, the chick was even faster. Granny's instinct was to put her wing over her baby and draw it to her warm body. This would be fine for an owl baby, but the chick's instincts were just the opposite. It wanted to do a few fast turns around the box and explore its new world. The last thing it wanted was a big wing getting in its way. Poor Granny. She tried again and again, only to have the chick dart between her legs and out the other side. She began to croak with excitement as the yellow blob dashed back and forth cheeping happily. It was a very funny sight, but our laughter was cut short when we remembered we didn't have anything suitable for a baby chick to eat. Why hadn't we thought of that before?

There was another hasty drive, this time to the nearest animal feed store. Larry was soon back with the bag of chick-starter mash, but he had forgotten to ask for instructions. "Just dump it in," he said, and I did. As the mash went into her nest, Granny leapt out with a loud croak, showering the chick and me with a great cloud of fine mash. I peered into the box and could just make out

the chick standing bewildered up to its knees in mash.

While Granny shook herself indignantly, I ran to fetch a freshly killed mouse as a peace offering. By the time I got back, the chick had discovered it was alone in the nest and set up a piercing squeal. Granny forgot the mash, grabbed the mouse and darted back to her babe. "Now all will be well," I told myself. "The chick has its mash, and Granny has her mouse, and I'll just take one more peek at them before I go."

Why do things never work out the way we plan? Granny never gave the little chicken time to eat the mash underfoot because she had other plans for her babe. Before my astonished eyes, she waded into her nest, pinned the mouse under her talons, tore off a tiny morsel and pushed it into the chick's open beak. Even more astonishing, the baby obviously liked the mouse and cheeped loudly for more. I was shocked. A meat-eating chicken?

Between Granny and the yellow monster, the first mouse was polished off in no time. Thus encouraged, Granny rooted around in the mash for one of the mice she had stored and soon dug up another treasure. This mouse quickly disappeared like the first. Its stomach full, the chick stopped its endless cheeping and fell fast asleep where it stood. My last view, as I crept away, was of mother Granny tenderly putting her wing over the little yellow ball and pulling it gently in to her breast.

While Granny contentedly brooded her chick downstairs, Larry and I had a worried discussion upstairs. Now that Granny had so skilfully laid an egg, hatched it and was now feeding and mothering a chick, what was next? Baby chicks have a way of turning into big chickens, not big owls. How.long would it be before even Granny began to notice that something was wrong? Just a few days? Or weeks? And how big would the chicken be by then? How long could the chicken stay healthy on such an unnatural diet? So many questions and no answers at all; we would just have to wait and see what happened.

By the end of the first week, it certainly seemed that a diet of mice was just the thing for a baby chick. It was also obvious that the chick was the apple of Granny's eye. We were astonished how quickly Granny seemed to accept having her baby run around the nest box in a very un-owl-like way. What about her instincts for taking care of

a blind and helpless baby owl? They were apparently
suppressed, for Granny looked as proud as could be at the
agile chick. We found it entertaining to watch her efforts
to catch up with her chick when she wanted to brood it,
since she never really succeeded unless it fell asleep.
Then mother and babe were the picture of contentment.

After that first week we stopped worrying about the
chick's health because in ten days it had more than
doubled in size. It was now obvious that it was never
going to show any interest in the mash, which still
littered the box, and we had a great time trying to get rid
of it without resorting to the vacuum cleaner. Three mice
a day were now vanishing into Granny and her chick, and
Granny was even calling me for more. I had not imagined
how complicated life would be as the mate of an owl and
the father of a chicken! I began to feel a lot of sympathy
for father owls out hunting in the woods while their
families screamed for food from the nest. At least I had a
mouse colony that supplied me with mice and kept Granny
from getting too bad-tempered.

Meanwhile, the chick gobbled up every shred of mouse
and grew like a balloon. It seemed livelier than ever, and
poor Granny was still trying to brood it, although the
only way she could slow it down was to knock it over with
her wing. Just when she would finally corner it, after a lot
of twisting and turning, the wretched thing would dash off
in another direction, scratch at some imagined remnant
of mouse and scoot away again. The nest box that had
once seemed so large now began to look too small for
both of them. Did I just imagine that Granny's nerves were
getting as frayed as her feathers, or was she still enjoying
the role of motherhood?

Soon a new pattern began to emerge, and it was even

more alarming. The chick, now rapidly becoming a chicken, was getting grabby about the mice. It had learned that mice appeared as if by magic at the door of the nest box, and it began to keep a sharp eye out for their arrival. One day, just as I handed a mouse to Granny–*zip*–the chicken darted forward, grabbed it and was off with its prize. The chicken ran from corner to corner, trying to peck off bits of the mouse before Granny, croaking like a bullfrog, caught up with it. Around and around they went, and with each turn, Granny's lovely feathers became more and more tattered. Her nest was a terrible mess too; it wasn't designed for a chicken chase.

One day, during just such a scuffle, the chicken flew right out of the door of the nest box, still holding grimly onto the mouse, and flopped onto the floor of the cage. Granny leaped right out after it, equally determined to take possession of the mouse. Once again the chase was on, and what a ridiculous sight it was to see a big, black and orange owl chasing a half-grown chicken around a cage on foot. The newspapers on the floor of the cage went flying in all directions, adding to the confusion. By

this time the chicken had dropped the mouse into the papers somewhere and was squawking as only a chicken can, with Granny in hot pursuit, croaking away.

"That," I said loudly, "is enough of that." I joined the chase, scooped up the chicken and carried it, still squawking, right out of the house. I put it into an outdoor enclosure to cool down. When I got back to Granny, she was sitting on the floor, breathless and bewildered, croaking forlornly in a sea of papers. Poor old owl, she looked a nervous wreck. What a way to end her first experience with motherhood.

I gathered her up tenderly and set her on her favourite perch. I tried to smooth her rumpled feathers, blowing softly into her neck and making soothing sounds. She began to stop puffing and slowly settled down while I went to fetch a nice fresh mouse, all for herself for a change. Later I saw her taking a long bath—the first real bath in weeks—and then she sat and preened her tattered feathers. I noticed she kept well away from the nest box, and we gave it a thorough cleaning the next day. I began to feel that she would soon recover her usual high spirits. One thing was certainly obvious; she didn't miss the chicken one bit. As for the chicken, we humanely put it to sleep.

The rest of the winter passed peacefully with Granny her old, cheerful self again. She had passed her first test of motherhood with flying colours. The fact that she had done it all with a chicken was not her fault. We had learned a great deal about owl instinct and behaviour from her. Now we were excited by the thought that perhaps next year, when we were better prepared for her annual event, we might be able to give her a motherless owl to look after.

"Have a good rest, Granny," I would say to her as she sat dozing on her perch behind my chair. "Save up your strength, because next time we have big plans for you." And she would open one orange eye and glare at me suspiciously for a moment. I don't know what winter dreams she had, if owls have dreams at all, but my daydreams were of mother Granny, resplendent in her new plumage, enthroned in a handsome new nest box. But this time she would surround an orphaned baby owl with all her gentleness and love, tenderly drawing it in to her soft breast.

Chapter 5
GRANNY, MILDRED AND POPS

After the episode of the chicken, Granny spent a peaceful spring and summer out of doors in her big flight cage. She shed her tattered old plumage and grew a full set of shiny new feathers. She spent a lot of time in her wide shallow pool, splashing around like a child. I wish I knew if she admired the flowering vines along one side of her cage, but what owls think about things, if they think at all, is a well-kept secret.

One thing she *was* interested in were the squirrels and chipmunks that sometimes wandered into her cage, only to find it was occupied by sharp claws and a snapping beak. Most of them escaped, but only by a whisker!

As summer changed into autumn, Granny began to call to me again. I could hear her familiar grunts and cackles even from the house, and when she saw me coming towards her cage, she would dive into the nearest roost box and make a noise like water going down a drain. I think she felt her unusual call was sure to attract her mate. Obviously her experience with the chicken had not put her off motherhood forever.

We brought Granny inside in November, and by Christmas she had been sitting on her latest egg for three weeks. Once again, it was an unfertilized egg, so it would never hatch. We worried about how disappointed she would be this year without even a chicken to mother, but neither of us could face that fiasco again. Luckily Granny's own instincts told her when it was time to give up on her egg and she started coming upstairs again in January. Little did either of us guess what was just about to happen.

One February night there was a terrible windstorm that blew big branches off the trees. It also blew down the old nest of a pair of Great Horned Owls in a woodlot not far away. The farmer who owned the woodlot went out to see the damage the next morning, and there on the ground was a fuzzy little white thing, shivering in the cold. It was also bleating as loudly as it could, so he picked it up and put it inside his shirt where it was warm. Then he took it to a Humane Society Shelter, and they called us.

We brought the tiny baby owl home in a box lined with cotton wool resting on a hot water bottle. As soon as we got it home, we put it in our hospital room. We covered the box with a dark towel to protect the baby's eyes and put the box under a heat lamp. We were relieved to see that it seemed like a sturdy little owlet. It even tried to sit up when we gave it a few drops of water and glucose. But we were certainly not prepared for what happened when it suddenly began to make tiny bleating cries from its cosy box.

Even though the owlet was in a different room, Granny could hear it. She nearly went crazy. First she looked in her box, just to make sure that her old egg hadn't hatched after all. Then she leapt out of her nest box and began crashing around in her cage, croaking like an old bullfrog again. She banged into the wooden bars of her cage, grabbed a stowed mouse, dropped it in her pool and generally went berserk. She *knew* there was a baby around somewhere, and she wanted it!

We had always hoped we could give Granny a real owl baby someday, but now that we had one we were afraid to risk it. What if the baby was too small for her and she stepped on it? What if she let it get cold? What if she gave it too big a piece of mouse and it choked? What if…? While we worried about these things we could hear Granny crashing around in her cage. "We'll have to chance it," said Larry. "We know Granny has all the right instincts to be a good mother." So we did.

Very apprehensively I picked up the tiny owlet and put

it in Granny's nest. The nest looked big and bare and cold after the cosy little box of cotton wool. The owlet was just a little bit of white fluff, blind and helpless, lying there on the pine needles. We held our breath. Granny sat still, watching me, and all was silent. Suddenly the most piteous bleat came from the nest—a high, squeaking, wavering bleat. Granny was at the nest in one leap, every feather standing on end. She stared into the nest for a moment and then stepped carefully down onto the pine needles. I just had to see, so I followed her to the box.

Why did we worry so much? Of course Granny knew exactly what to do and how to do it! She tip-toed around the baby, oh so carefully, and planted her big feet one on either side of it. Slowly she sank down over the little form, her thick breast feathers falling around it like a soft curtain. As if by magic the owlet stopped its unhappy chittering, and Granny, a mother once more, bent her head down to groom her new baby.

After a while we took Granny a fresh mouse because we knew the baby needed to be fed. She tucked the mouse under one foot and, without raising herself from the baby, began to pull off tiny strips of meat. Suddenly a little head wobbled out from under her breast feathers and the morsel of food was transferred to the owlet's soft beak.

Naturally, with Granny's excellent care, the owlet thrived and grew. When it was about ten days old, I lifted it out of her nest to be weighed and measured. It was a fat, soft, fluffy little mound of white, with one eye half open and long silken eye lashes. There was something faintly ridiculous about this tubby little owlet who looked in our general direction with lop-sided indignation. We christened it Mildred because it was much too feminine to ever turn out to be a boy owl. We wanted to take a picture of her but Granny was beginning to huff and puff so we had to put her back. Granny fussed over her as if we had done something dreadful.

And so the days passed, Granny in heaven and Mildred eating like a pig. But owlets don't stay little for long, and soon Mildred was too big to fit under Granny's breast. Instead she now sat beside Granny. I kept trying to get a good look at Mildred, but Granny held her wing over her baby and all I could glimpse was a fat belly, fuzzy legs and big feet.

As long as Mildred stayed leaning up against Granny, we knew we didn't have to worry about how far and how clearly the owlet was able to see. Her eyes still had a bluish colour to the pupils, a sort of milkiness that goes away as vision develops. But we kept watching for the signs of clear vision as Mildred neared her third week and began to move her head from side to side like a Balinese dancer. This is the first real indication that an owlet is beginning to see clearly. It is a sign that the owlet is trying to tell how near or how far things are.

Like any young owl, Mildred began to watch anxiously for her mother whenever Granny hopped out of the box for a few minutes. At first all Mildred could see was just a blur as Granny approached the nest, but at least it was a blur that made familiar, comforting sounds. Soon we knew that Mildred would also begin to recognize the way Granny looked, as her eyes focussed more sharply. Then the problems would begin.

If we left them together too long, Mildred would "imprint" on Granny—she would think she was a Spectacled Owl like Granny instead of a Great Horned Owl. Then, if she met a Great Horned Owl like herself, she would be frightened by it. We knew how owls act when an unfamiliar owl approaches. They click their beaks and raise their wings and sway from side to side, trying to look very

ferocious and hoping the strange owl will be scared away.
We didn't want Mildred to be frightened by her own kind. We
wanted to raise her to be a normal Great Horned Owl who
could live with her own kind back in the wild. So you can see
why we were so anxious that she didn't get accustomed to
the way Granny looked. We also had to be careful that

Mildred didn't see very much of us either, because it would
be just as damaging to her future life with Great Horned Owls
if she got the idea that people were what her species looked
like!

So while we sneaked past Granny's cage, trying to see
what was happening in Granny's nest without being seen by
Mildred, we puzzled about how we could introduce the little
owlet to another Great Horned Owl when the time came.
We could see Mildred leaning out of the nest, peering
anxiously around in the soft light, trying to see where
mother Granny had gone, and we knew we didn't have very
long to come up with a solution.

We decided that our only real hope was a Great Horned
Owl we called Pops, who lived outside in one of our big flight
cages. Heaven knows why we had called him Pops, but as it
turned out we couldn't have picked a better name for this
wonderful owl.

Chapter 6
POPS, AN OWL SUPERSTAR

P ops is a Great Horned Owl, the same species as little Mildred, and in his own way he is just as amazing as Granny. He is also just as handsome, but Pops and Granny look so different it is difficult to believe they are both owls. Pops is about 46 cm/18 inches from his tail to his head and there are another 8 cm/3 inches of ear tufts above that. He has a white ruff under his beak and fine bands of black and white across his breast. His cheeks, head and wings are a rich tawny colour, edged in black. His talons and beak are black, and his eyes are big golden circles.

Pops came to us when he was about three months old. He had never seen anything but people, so it was much too late to convince him that he was an owl. Because he was such a mixed-up bird, he couldn't be released back into the wild, but neither could we keep such a big owl in the house. We had to put him out in a large flight cage with some other Great Horned Owls, but not knowing they were his species, it must have been a lonely life for him.

Then one spring we made an amazing discovery. We had just received a young Great Horned Owl with a broken leg, and we had to put its leg in a splint for two weeks. Because we wanted the young owl to see its own kind while its leg was healing, we hung its hospital cage outside the big cage so it could see other Great Horned Owls. The little cage had a tiny door through which we could push mice.

When it saw all those adult Horned Owls sitting there in the big cage, the juvenile instinctively began to call for food. It knew that they were its species, and it obviously felt they should be doing something about fetching food. The next day, when I came along with the basket of mice, what should I see but Pops, perched on a branch beside the little cage. He was trying to push one of his mice through the wire to the owlet. Needless to say, the juvenile was in whole-hearted agreement with this effort and was doing its best to grab the incoming end of the mouse. It was also keeping up a constant squeal of encouragement.

What a fantastic sight! I could hardly believe my own eyes when I reflected that Pops had just sat forlornly in a corner of the big cage for the last three years, keeping well away from the others.

Could it be that his behaviour was triggered by instinct when he heard the owlet calling for food? We knew that Pops had never had the experience of being a father himself. To test his instinct, we started giving all the juvenile's mice to Pops, along with his own. He never let us down. In fact, he was such a diligent provider that he often gave the owlet his own mice too!

As soon as we could take off its splint, we moved the young owl into the big cage with Pops. By the end of the first day the juvenile had climbed onto the big platform in Pops' corner and was hreeping for food while poor Pops leaped back and forth like a yo-yo between the food box and the platform.

That juvenile learned to fly around the cage and pick up its own food, and it was soon released back into the wild. Watching Pops take care of the young owl had taught us a valuable lesson about imprinting. Even though Pops had imprinted on people and didn't recognize other adult Horned Owls, he hadn't lost his instinct to feed food-crying young Horned Owls.

Now you can see why we thought of our wonderful Pops when it was time for little Mildred to leave Granny's tender care and meet an owl of her own species. But

there was a problem. Unlike the injured juvenile, Mildred was much too young to be outside without a mother to keep her warm. This meant that Pops would have to come inside. He hadn't been inside for three years, and it might upset him so much that he wouldn't do anything useful. We decided to risk it.

We knew we'd have to build a special cage for this experiment, but where? Then we remembered a small unfinished room under the stairs. We cut a big window in the door and another in the wall. We fastened bamboo curtains over these, so we could see in but the owls couldn't see out. Then we hung a platform nest on one wall and put a perch for Pops against the opposite wall.

When we were done we took a deep breath and went out and captured Pops. He was highly indignant, but we left him in the room overnight with two fresh mice. So far so good. We heard him call once during the night and he sounded pretty forlorn. Little did he know what was coming.

The day of the big experiment dawned. First I laid two medium-sized mice on the floor in plain view of Pops. Then I went to Granny's nest, and as she began her bullfrog imitation, I lifted out little Mildred. I felt like a kidnapper. Quickly I placed Mildred on the platform opposite Pops and closed the door. We peeked through the bamboo curtains. It was hard to concentrate because of Granny. She was making heart-rending sounds from the other room, but Mildred's future was too important to go to Granny now. After we found out if it was going to work, we could comfort Granny.

So we watched, not daring to make a sound. Mildred and Pops faced each other, and all was still in the little room. Then, slowly at first, Mildred began to sway from side to side as she tried to focus on Pops. He blinked once or twice and she swayed faster. Did she wonder what that funny looking thing was? Could she tell it looked a lot different from Granny? Did this new thing have something to do with food? She gave a lusty hreeep, just in case. Poor Granny heard the call, and we could hear the bullfrog noise starting up again. Now Mildred was *sure* she was going to be fed, so she put her whole heart and soul into her food calls. It was deafening.

Apparently it was too much for Pops. With an air of

real desperation he leapt down from his perch, seized a mouse, jumped up to the platform and shoved it into Mildred's beak. We were almost as delighted as Mildred. When she recovered from her surprise, she tried the magic noise again, and Pops leapt down to the mouse and delivered it like the first. Having a full stomach is the most important thing in the world to an owlet. If Mildred remembered Granny at all, she soon forgot her in the satisfaction of having this big bird waiting on her hand and foot.

Since Pops was the only moving object Mildred could see, it took less than ten days for her to imprint on his appearance. I knew our experiment had worked the day I opened the door to clean Pops' and Mildred's room and Mildred nearly had a fit at the sight of me. I was definitely *not* a familiar object, and she snapped at me and fanned her wings and blinked her eyes, backing slowly away.

We were so delighted with our success that we moved her outside with Pops to his big cage. Like the owlet he had looked after earlier, she sat on his platform and directed his every move. After that it was only a short time before she too was flying all around the cage, taking her own food and totally independent of Pops. While Granny and Pops went back to their own routines, we introduced Mildred to two other half-grown Great Horned Owls. Together they learned to catch live mice and were released in a lovely big woodlot a few miles away. This is the end of our story about Mildred, but it was not the end of Pops' adventures as a father.

Two years later, three baby Great Horned Owls arrived at the same time. They were just at the age when they were beginning to see, so we bypassed Granny and put them straight into the little room with Pops. He looked a little more upset than usual when he saw how many there were. After all, he'd only worked with babies one at a time before.

The three babes sat on the nest looking suspiciously at this weird creature across from them. Pops stared grimly back at them. One by one, they began to weave around on the platform, doing their Balinese dancer act, heads bobbing and swaying. Pops shifted his feet nervously. Inevitably, one of the babes tried a hreeep. Then another tried one, and soon, encouraged by each other, they were bleating and squawking as only young owls can. Poor Pops knew what that sound meant. He frantically grabbed a mouse and stuffed it into the gaping beak nearest the edge of the nest. The owlets were just thrilled by this gratifying turn of events. They set up a piercing symphony of trills and squeals and struggled for the position nearest the edge. Sure enough, Pops leapt onto the nest with another mouse, and the owlets nearly fell off in delight.

By this time the clamour was deafening, and Pops was dashing back and forth. When the mice were all eaten, he got back on his perch a safe distance from the nest. For a few moments it was actually quiet as the babies stared at him, unable to believe dinner was over. Then they set up a terrible wailing, hreeping din and fell to quarrelling amongst themselves. Pops sat stonily on his perch. Fortunately for all of us, the uproar soon subsided and the three owlets, stomachs full, began to topple over in sleep.

Year after year Pops lives up to his name and sees his charges safely through to independence. Whatever would we do without him? He is a real superstar, and many Horned Owls out in the wild owe their freedom to him.

Chapter 7
TIGLET, A RESIDENT MENACE

Tiglet is a Screech Owl—a silly name for a species with such a lovely song. Screech Owls are small compared with owls like Granny or Pops, but what they lack in size they more than make up for in nerve. Tiglet is a good example of how much character can fit into one small owl. He is a tyrant, a fierce enemy, a tireless rival and a great lover. He is sure that I am his mate and that poor Larry is his rival. He never stops trying to drive Larry from what Tiglet considers to be his own territory, which is the house. *All* of the house!

Although Tiglet is an adult now, he is still only 15cm/6 inches tall. He is a beautiful blend of black and white and grey feathers, with yellow eyes and little black ear tufts. But the first time we saw Tiglet he was a tiny speck of white fluff about four days out of an egg. He was found behind a tent, one rainy May evening, by boys camping in a woods not far from us. The trees overhead were towering oaks, far too high for the campers to try to return the baby to its nest, so the boys' parents brought the owl to us.

That was ten years ago. In those days we didn't have all the foster parent owls we have now, so we knew we would have to raise the baby ourselves. And we knew it would grow up thinking that humans were its own kind. At least, we thought, Screech Owls are small enough so that they can get adequate exercise in a house. Little did we know what a mess one small owl can make.

It all began innocently enough. Tiglet grew rapidly and graduated from an incubator to a padded nest in a portable box and then to a cosy little nest box fastened to the wall of a big cage. This cage was in the perfect place for a nosy little owl like Tiglet, who liked to see everything that went on. The cage was once an attic storeroom, high up under the peaked roof of our house, over my bathroom. We put a skylight overhead and cut out big areas of the room's walls to make screened windows so that Tiglet could look down into the living room, bedroom and two hallways.

We also cut a trap door in the floor of the cage leading into the top shelf of my bathroom cupboard. Finally, we cut a little round hole in the face of this cupboard. The bathroom led to the bedroom and the rest of the house. By the time Tiglet was four months old, he could get a pretty good fix on the action anywhere in the house from his eyrie, and he could take a corner pretty fast when he was on his way out of his cage to mischief or escaping back into his lair.

He was an irresistible little waif, so bright and affectionate and busy. Especially busy. I must have a hundred pictures of Tiglet: sitting in an indoor tree, its bark hanging in strips; in the act of pulling leaves off houseplants; defecating down the lamp-shades; dropping his pellets into our mugs of tea; bathing in the dogs' water dish; shredding only the best books; and sitting in the middle of what was once a nice dried flower arrangement. The list is endless, and all of it is bad. But how could we be cross with such a sweet little ball of fluff with such outrageous eyelashes?

For several months we even let him into the bedroom during the night, but he was thrown out when he developed an extra-ordinary habit. Tiglet loved company, and when he looked down and saw us getting into bed, it was more than he could resist. He would arrive on my pillow with a soft thud and snuggle up to my ear, making low, sweet bleats of contentment. Dear little owl, I would think, as I stroked his silken head. Those were such cosy moments, and he never once soiled the bedding. But Tiglet could never leave well enough alone. Soon he would move over to Larry's pillow and sit, fascinated by something, as Larry slowly drifted into sleep. I couldn't be sure what he was watching so closely, but it seemed to be Larry's bristly moustache. In fact, Tiglet seemed to be leaning right over the moustache for some reason.

A dreadful roar shattered the quiet night as Larry lifted off the bed, his arms flailing. Tiglet fled to the bathroom and the safety of his cage, and I stared at Larry open-mouthed. He seemed to be holding his upper lip. "What the Hell was that?" he asked, looking around for a wasp. But I knew it was no wasp. Tiglet had pounced on Larry's moustache and pulled with all his might. Did Tiglet think the moustache was a mouse? I offered this explanation,

but Larry was in no mood for humour. He marched over to
the bathroom and slammed the door shut behind Tiglet.

A week or so later, when I was reading in bed, Tiglet
once again flew onto my pillow for a little snuggle. What a
charming little creature he was, I thought. Then, like an
iron filing drawn by a magnet, he slowly advanced on
Larry's sleeping form. I know I should have shooed Tiglet
away at that point, but my curiosity got the better of my
judgement. So I watched. Slowly and carefully Tiglet
neared the irresistible moustache, huddling over it as
before and stretching out his neck. I leaned closer to get
a better look. In a flash Tiglet had seized one bristly hair
and pulled. So *that* was it—he was trying to pull an

earthworm out of the ground, his talons braced against Larry's cheek.

The bed covers erupted again, Larry's roar more terrible than the first time. His upswinging arm caught Tiglet in mid-air and knocked him to the floor. "Where is that...owl," he yelled, as Tiglet scuttled across the floor to the bathroom. "What kind of a nut-house is this, anyway?" I pulled the covers over my head, unable to stop laughing, and heard the bathroom door slammed shut once again.

After that episode I dared not let Tiglet back into the bedroom, although he continued to wing around the house in the evenings. As the months passed Tiglet became more accustomed to being with me than Larry, who was often in his office with his grilled door closed. By the end of the year he had stopped seeing me as his mother and now considered me his mate. And that meant Larry was his rival! Like a wild owl, Tiglet began trying to drive his rival from his territory.

Tiglet's tactics did nothing to endear him to Larry. The little monster would lie in wait for Larry in dark hallways, and as Larry passed innocently beneath, Tiglet would give him a sharp blow on the back of his head. It was infuriating enough when Larry was empty-handed, but when he was carrying a mug of hot tea it was disastrous. In self-defense, Larry took to wearing a hard hat around the house and threatened to carry a club as well.

Tiglet didn't confine his "clearing the territory of rivals" to my tormented husband. Visitors were attacked as well, whenever and wherever they were encountered. Suddenly a grey feathered fury would swoop down from nowhere, all beak and talons. Larry began to keep watch over his shoulders, in a furtive way, checking out the dark ledges for yellow eyes and shiny claws.

Even our dogs were not immune. We had a large, shaggy grey Scottish Deerhound called Morag, who liked to spend her evenings sprawled across the living room rug. Unfortunately, this put Morag in the middle of one of Tiglet's longest flight paths, between a dining room picture frame and a living room bookcase. Out of the corner of my eye I would see the grey marauder streaking through the doorway. Lower and lower he would fly until, with his legs down and forward as the strike occurred, Tiglet swept on towards the bookcase with a tuft of grey fur!

Watching the reactions of a sleeping Deerhound is like seeing a movie in slow motion. Poor Morag had to gather in her long legs from all over the place, get them folded under her and then lurch to her feet. When all of this was accomplished, she would snap indignantly at the empty air, glare suspiciously at each of us in turn and get sulkily up onto a chair where she could keep a careful eye on us. Meanwhile, rotten Tiglet piously combed the grey fur out of his beak. I always suspected he was secretly laughing at us.

Last spring, when Tiglet was ten years old, we moved him to a beautiful cage outside our bedroom window. It had been a sundeck, and we had screened it in and covered the floor with sand. In his new home, Tiglet has big plants and high perches and two roost boxes, one of which leads into a tunnel to our bedroom. It took Tiglet a few days to get over being afraid of all the space beyond the screen, but the exciting calls of other Screech Owls in the compounds below soon kept him fully occupied. I'm sure he doesn't know they are Screech Owls; he just responds to the right song.

This spring we introduced Tiglet to his first wild baby, a little grey squeaker that was just old enough to leave the nest. Young birds at this stage are called "fledgelings." We set the fledgeling on a branch in Tiglet's cage. It hung on for dear life until it caught sight of Tiglet. Then it forgot about everything except squealing for food. Tiglet endured the racket for about twenty minutes, then he picked up one of the tiny mice I'd provided and, looking bewildered by his own instinctive actions, offered it to the fat little owlet. Like all babies, the owlet wolfed it down and squealed for more.

It is the beginning of a new life for our Tiglet. Now he will be a foster father to other Screech Owls, just as Pops has been to baby Great Horned Owls. Besides, after ten years of fooling around, it was high time Tiglet started to work!

Chapter 8
I REMEMBER
MAMA-SAN

W hen I hear people who don't know anything about owls refer to them as vicious creatures, I think of all the gentle, patient owls I have known over the years. And most of all, I remember Mama-San. The gentlest of the gentle, she fostered wild babies until she was old and nearly blind.

Her story may be sad in some ways, but it is also a story of hope and success. She was a Screech Owl from Canada's west coast, and unlike the other owls you have met, she was badly injured in a collision with a car. She had a broken leg and wing and a destroyed eye. For six months she was hospitalized indoors, while her leg healed and her wing mended enough for her to fly for short hops. Her eye dried up and stayed clear of infection, and we were delighted to find she had enough sight in her good eye to see where she was going.

Finally we moved her outside, into the soft air of early spring, to a big cage inhabited by a beautiful, copper-coloured bachelor Screech Owl. It was love at first sight, maybe because he had lived alone for several years or just because it was spring. Whatever the reason, there was a kind of magic between them, despite the fact that their songs were so different. Two months after they first met, she was in a nest box on three eggs. After years of waiting for our first Screech Owl brood, we could hardly believe it.

In due course tell-tale, reedy, whinnying calls came from the nest box, and Ginger (the father) was kept on the jump supplying mice to Mama-San and her babies. When the two beautiful, fuzzy little babies came out of the box they were about three weeks old and a lovely blend of copper and grey. They were inseparable, almost as if they were physically attached. They looked like little gnomes with their big feet and eyes, and Ginger and Mama-San were filled with pride.

We hid when we watched the little family so that the babies would not see us. We were pleased to think that at least these little owls could be raised by their natural parents.

Tragically, our beautiful Ginger was killed by a weasel late in the summer, after his owlets were eating on their own. We were devastated, not only because we had known him for a long time, but also because we grieved for Mama-San and her brief romance. Would we ever find another mate for her?

In the fall we tore down Ginger's cage and rebuilt it so that no weasels could get in. It was designed as two big separate areas with a connecting corridor. We put Mama-San in one territory and a very small male named Rusty in the other. Rusty was almost two years old and had never been a father. He had collided with a car as a juvenile and was stone deaf in one ear. Rusty was a nervous little owl.

All winter these two eyed each other across the courtyard of their cage. In the early spring we removed the partition in the corridor between them, then hid behind some shrubs to see what they did. We waited and waited, but absolutely nothing happened. Day after day, Mama-San stayed in her territory and Rusty stayed in his. We were very disappointed after our quick success with Ginger. Then we realized that we had not heard Rusty vocalizing the way Ginger had done in early spring. Without his song there was nothing to lure Mama-San down the corridor. Perhaps Rusty was silent because he was half deaf and couldn't hear the other male Screech Owls calling to their mates.

Then in early May I realized I had not seen Mama-San for a day or so and I went into her territory to investigate. She wasn't in view, and she wasn't in Rusty's half either. Mystified, I got a ladder to look into her box. There she was, sitting on two eggs. We watched Rusty for any sign of involvement, but he just stayed home looking at the scenery. After four weeks we were about to take away the useless eggs when we had a bright idea. We had received several orphaned Screech Owls that spring, and two were still nestlings. Would Mama-San be a foster mother like Granny?

We put them in her box a little apprehensively, but she just accepted them as if suddenly finding two nestlings in her silent box was the most natural thing in the world. I could hear the contented little squeaks and rustlings, but dared I take a peek? I decided to have one quick look, and sure enough, there were all three of them leaning on each other. Mama-San, with her good eye closed, was grooming the face of the baby against her breast.

But it was Rusty's reaction that really surprised us. While Mama-San had been sitting on her eggs, occasionally calling for food, he had stayed resolutely in his own territory, even though we knew he wasn't deaf in *both* ears. Now suddenly he began to pay nervous attention to the ruckus in the next territory. Mama-San had had to fetch her own mice while she was on the unfertilized eggs, but now that she had babies she must have instinctively felt there should be a father around. So she indignantly added her voice to the bleating calls of the babies. The racket in the box increased in volume and urgency, and Rusty began to fidget and hop around his cage.

We had put extra mice in his food box, just in case, and now he came nervously down the connecting corridor with one in his beak. After a long pause, he hopped up onto a perch in Mama-San's half and paused again. Clearly he was scared. Then he flew a little closer, and Mama-San's calls grew even louder. Finally he got up the nerve to hop onto the perch outside the nest box, and while he was gathering his courage for the final approach, Mama-San stuck her

head out the door and seized his mouse.

After that, Rusty was an ardent supplier of mice, growing braver with each trip to her box. When those foster owlets were launched into independence, Rusty and Mama-San remained good friends. As you might expect, the following spring they had two babies of their own—this time both grey like their mother. And just for good measure we gave her another foster baby to raise as well. By this time, Rusty

didn't care which food box the mice came from, just as long as there were plenty of them and his family was fed.

Their nest box was a busy place each spring for several happy years. Mama-San produced two or three babies each year and raised two or three foster nestlings as well. Then suddenly, following the moult one summer, she produced a lot of white feathers all over her body. This is a sure sign of advancing age in an owl, just as white hair is in a person. We were sad to see this sign because we knew what it meant, and all through the cold weather that winter we watched her anxiously to make sure she was all right.

By spring Mama-San couldn't see her food unless we put dark mice on a very light background, and we realized that she was almost totally blind. Because of her crippled wing, she had always been more of a climber than a flyer. Now, despite her blindness, she got around her cage quite well by climbing on familiar branches, but she seemed to have forgotten how to reach her nest box. Pathetically, she dropped an egg onto the ground in late April, and our hearts were sore to see her nearing the end of her life. Did we only imagine it or was there something sad and forlorn in her appearance as well?

As a last attempt to give her something happy to do, I put two little Screech Owls in her territory. They were at the age when they could perch on branches but not find their own food. Heading for the constant bleating noises they made, she found them, and she stuck to them like glue. Rusty swung into action again. He not only fed the babies, but Mama-San as well.

Even though her life was almost over, Mama-San somehow looked almost happy again, now that she felt important to someone. Owls, like people, are happiest when they are busy, and our much-loved Mama-San seemed to be rejuvenated by having owlets needing her once more. If only we could have told her what a wonderful owl she was and how much we needed her....

She left a big hole in our hearts when she was gone. She must have raised a lot of babies through all the springtimes of her life, and she gave a chance at life to seven foster babies as well. I like to imagine that they are still living out there in the wild, a final testament to her devotion.

Chapter 9
SOOK,
A FLYING STOMACH

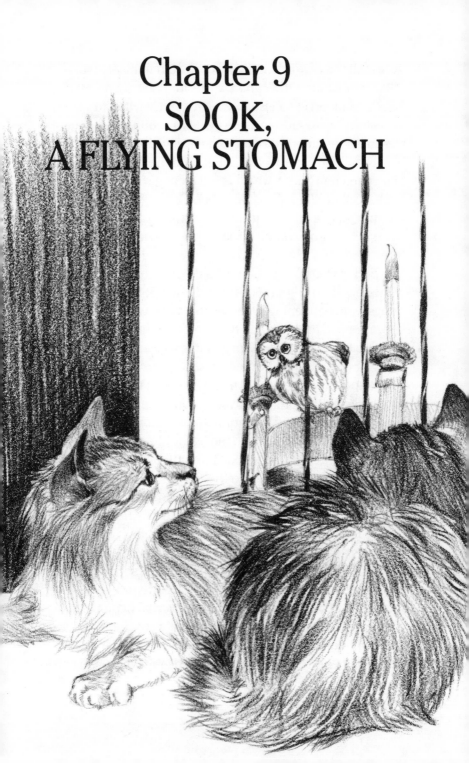

S mall is the word for Sook, who could fit nicely into a coffee mug. Other good words for Sook are nervy, piggy and incorrigible. He is a Saw-Whet Owl, the littlest owl in eastern North America, and he has a round head without ear-tufts, cinnamon coloured plumage, yellow eyes and a black beak. He came from Quebec, and the family who raised him called him Sucre, which is the French word for sweet. We have simplified his name to Sook.

His Quebec family showed us pictures of him as a baby, when he was an adorable little ball of brown fluff with a dark brown face and white eyebrows. They even had a picture of him riding around their house on the back of an old, deaf, white cat. This all sounds like great fun, but two serious things were happening. One was that Sook was firmly imprinting on humans, and the other was that he was learning to think of cats as playmates—a very dangerous habit for an owl when he meets a strange cat.

As soon as Sook started flying he began to leave his droppings on the family's furniture. Unfortunately, birds can't be house-trained, and the family soon discovered that living with an owl was not as much fun as they had expected. But they were fond of him and didn't want to put him in a canary cage for the rest of his life, so they began to think of either letting him go or finding another home for him. Fortunately, they called our centre, and we told them why he could never be released and that we would try to give him a life with some purpose. Sook was three months old when he arrived.

What an irresistible little gnome he was, so bright-eyed and frisky, with soft, velvety feathers. He was already a good flier and had begun to develop the nocturnal habits of his species, which meant he needed a quiet roost for the daylight hours. We had a big cage for him up under a skylight in our front hall. The cage had grapevines hanging in the corners, and Sook perched in among them. He could hide in these secret places so completely that we could barely see him as he rested up for his evening exercise.

Before we consigned him to living with people forever we wanted to make absolutely sure there was no hope that Sook would recognize his own kind. A week after he arrived, we brought in a mature female from one of our outside compounds and put her in his cage. The poor unsuspecting female had just hopped up to a nice perch in a secluded corner and was settling down for the day when a feathered bomb hit her amidships and knocked her off the perch. We couldn't believe our eyes! Plainly, neither could she when she looked around and discovered her attacker was a mere baby, an owlet she had hardly bothered to notice when she first entered the cage. From his expression of open hostility, it was clear that Sook was planning a second attack.

She stared up at him (we *all* stared up at him) and sure enough, buzzing like an enraged bee, he came at her again. This time she got out of his way and he hit the pine needles on the floor of the cage. Now he was madder than ever, and he gathered himself up and turned to face her, every feather standing on end. They were only a few inches apart and before we could intervene, he went for her again, both feet clutching. But this time she was ready for him. She had recovered from the shock of being attacked by a male, and just a baby at that (two things that would never happen with a normal owl), and she was going to teach him a lesson. We had to rescue Sook because he would be no match for an indignant adult female. But he came out kicking and screaming and full of fight.

Now that it was obvious Sook had no idea what his own species looked like, we decided to just relax and enjoy him. But to enjoy sharing our house with a mischievous little owl like Sook was not easy. Consider his baby notions about cats, for instance. Sook thought cats were playthings, something for owls to land on. It took a few nasty encounters for him to learn that our cats were young and spry and thought that owls were a form of cat food. But Sook was such a little demon that he liked to live dangerously. He could never resist diving at the cats and then giving them the raspberry, a rude buzzing sound, after he reached a safe perch. He nearly drove the cats mad.

Because his actions seem so suicidal to us, we have developed an evening routine. Before we open his cage, we make sure the cats have climbed up the ladder to their own nest, a grilled box at the top of the broom closet where they like to sleep the evenings away. Once they are safely inside, we close their grilled door. Next, Tiglet, the Screech Owl, follows me downstairs to spend his evenings flying around and "owl watching" the new arrivals in the convalescent cages. Then I bring Granny upstairs to her roost behind my desk chair. Finally, we lock the outside doors. Now it is time for Sook to come out.

The very first thing Sook does is check out the cats. He perches on the dining room chandelier and stares fixedly into the cats' nest through the grilled door. If they are still awake, they stare back at him and lick their chops. If they are asleep, he gives them the raspberry, which always brings them to full alert. Now that he has ruined their sleep and got them pacing back and forth, he flies off with a little smart-alec flourish and does a few fast turns around the rest of the house. As soon as the cats have settled down again, he is back on the chandelier, buzzing at them once more. Some owls just can't bear to leave things alone, and Sook is a natural agitator.

When he isn't making the cats' lives miserable, Sook finds

other pastimes. One is scaring us with his aerial acrobatics. He flies at the stone chimney in the living room at full throttle. Just as we picture him as an owl pancake, splatted against the stone, he does a vertical climb up the chimney, followed by a daredevil roll off the top and lands on an iron lamp just below the ceiling. Then he fixes me with his golden stare as much as to say, "Now, lets see *you* do that!"

It took us a while to learn what these feathered bees can do. Sook will follow me down the bedroom hall, just above my head. If I open a door that he doesn't want to fly through, he will hang there in the air for a few seconds, with his wings in reverse prop, hovering like a helicopter. Then he'll zoom off at a right angle back down the hall.

Sook's flying abilities are equalled only by his curiosity, and the only thing more insatiable than his curiosity is his appetite. If there is a ruling passion in Sook's life, other than making the cats' lives miserable, it is his passion for a fat little mouse. Everything that goes on in this house is monitored by him, on the chance that it will have something to do with mice. I guess this instinct is pretty important to a little owl out making his living in the woods.

If I am at my desk and Sook is nowhere to be seen, I have only to open a drawer and he will be there, all shiny-eyed and hopeful, just in case there is a mouse inside it. If Larry goes out to the kitchen, Sook will be overhead, hovering, watching and ready to pounce should a brown furry thing suddenly materialize from thin air. Since Sook has never seen a live mouse in the kitchen, we have to wonder at his persistence. Perhaps it is just his hunting instinct coupled with his observation that people and mice are usually found together.

When I clean our mouse colony in the evening, I have come to accept that Sook will be part of the ritual. There is

no hope at all of sneaking downstairs without him. He is usually at the door before I am, hovering, waiting to see if I'm really going down into the mouse room. There are other reasons why I might go downstairs, but Sook has an unerring sense of the times that will have something to do with mice. He is no help at all in the mouse colony. I dare not leave a cage uncovered even for an instant, or he will be into it, madly footing the hysterical mice.

He is allowed to perch on the cage lids, which he does, peering in, quivering with emotion at the sight of the scurrying forms, his eyes bulging at the spectacle below. He has often been bitten on his toes by indignant father mice, so he has taken to hopping around on the wire covers, never staying in one place long enough for the mice to take revenge. Owls have memories for many things, and Sook has a strong memory for mouse reprisals.

Every night around midnight, we lure Sook back to his own cage. We would probably never be able to get him into his cage were it not for his anticipation of a mouse dinner.

Usually we give him a live mouse. I have to keep it from him until I reach his cage and toss it in. Sook is never more than a few seconds behind, flying flat out and seizing it before it even lands on the floor. Fortunately, he kills mice more quickly and humanely than any human ever could.

Next, I lure Tiglet upstairs. He follows me and another mouse down the hall to his cage. Unlike Sook, Tiglet does not like to see his dinner running around, so I have to kill his mouse first. Granny is next to go downstairs to her cage for the night. She is the only owl who is allowed to be in the same part of the house as Sook, because she seems to regard him as no more than a tiresome fly who buzzes around, stirs up the air and ruffles her feathers. Sometimes she grunts at him, but she can't be bothered chasing him. I'm sure he instinctively knows this, and he just can't resist showing off right under her nose, whirling his wings, making her duck and buzzing off before she can give him a fast smack with her foot. Then Granny looks at me, reprovingly, as if to ask why I don't do something about that little twerp.

Last to be settled for the night are the two cats, now stirring impatiently in their nest. They come warily down the ladder, checking out the chandelier and any owl-frequented ledges, always hoping I have forgotten an owl, preferably the one that's very small. Then they go and check out Sook's cage, just in case the door isn't closed. But it always is closed, and safely behind it is the little demon. He sits high on a perch wiping his beak and arranging his feathers, deliberately waiting until he has their undivided attention before he leans over and gives them one last raspberry for the night!

Chapter 10
CRICKET, A DIFFERENT OWL

G ranny and Tiglet and Sook are not the only owls that live right in the house with us. Our other roommate is Cricket, a Burrowing Owl. Burrowing Owls don't look like any other kind of owl in the whole world. They are small with flat-topped heads and ridiculously long bare legs. Their tails are very short so they don't get in the way when the owl stands up straight on flat ground.

Cricket was hatched in an underground chamber just like a ground-hog's burrow. Although Burrowing Owls take over old gopher or badger holes in the wild, Cricket was hatched in one of five burrows we built in an enormous experimental compound. We had built this compound for three pairs of damaged Burrowing Owls from the western plains that we hoped to breed.

It was a special challenge to keep these owls outdoors over winter because normally they would have migrated to the warm southern states to escape the cold. But our biggest challenge was to build burrows that looked like abandoned gopher or badger burrows so the owls would feel at home. We built imitation burrows out of drainage pipe sections laid on top of electric heating cables buried inside mounds of sand. This way the tunnels stayed warm in winter and dry in spring. Outside their burrows we piled mounds of earth, placed big rocks and dug in cedar posts, all for lookout perches for these prairie owls.

Cricket's parents came from Idaho, and last spring, after their first winter in the big cage, they had their very first brood of seven beautiful owlets. We didn't see the babies until two weeks after they hatched, but we knew something was going on because the parents had dragged dried grasses into their tunnels and the father was very excited about mice. As soon as we put mice into the food box he would grab one and scoot down the nearest burrow opening,

only to emerge from the other end a few seconds later. If we listened carefully, we could hear the mother calling for food from deep inside the tunnel, and pretty soon we could hear the wheezing calls of the babies too.

When the oldest baby was two weeks old it began to wander along the tunnels and peek out in amazement,

bobbing and twisting its head as it looked around at the
outside world. To watch these activities, we had to hide
behind big cherry trees outside the compound and look
through binoculars. We were too far away for the owlet to
see us, but his parents nearly had a fit at being spied on in
this way. When they spotted us, both parents would fly from

post to post in their territory, bobbing up and down, squawking and shrilling at us as we skulked from tree to tree. It didn't take much of this racket to make the baby shrink back into the tunnel. He couldn't *see* what all the fuss was about, but he got the message that it was something pretty bad!

It became almost impossible to approach the cage unseen to count the babies. One of the adults always saw us first and gave the alarm. Then there would be a fast-moving blur of fuzzy blobs on sticklike legs, all trying to get into the tunnel at the same time. Even though we were annoyed, we had to admit it was a funny sight. It must be very difficult to sneak up on a Burrowing Owl in the prairies where there are no trees to hide behind.

It wasn't long before the seven little owlets were running across the grass, squabbling over possession of the rocks and posts and trying to stand on one leg the way their parents do. And soon they were all flying strongly around the big compound and learning to use some of the other tunnels we had built, especially as autumn approached.

Early this spring, we fed them for a month on live mice and crickets and shipped them out to a big ranch in British Columbia, where the government biologists had made careful preparations for their release. They had built nine burrows into the rolling hills of the ranch so our little owls would have a home right away and wouldn't have to wander off looking for a safe tunnel. One of the biologists lived nearby and went out on horseback each day to take the owls some fresh mice while they were getting used to their new homes. How I would love to see them in their freedom, in all that open space.

Meanwhile, back in Ontario, the parents of that first brood were busy with their second family. It wasn't long after the yearlings went to B.C. that we began to hear those telltale little sounds from the burrow again. And then the busy little father swung into action, grabbing mice and scurrying into the tunnel as the mother's impatient chirps mixed with the wheezing of the new infants.

But this year something very unusual happened. The first baby out of the tunnel broke his leg. In the morning he was running around on two legs, and at feeding time he was dragging one of them. It was a real emergency—we had to catch him before the bones poked through the skin. But how? We couldn't dig up the burrow with all those younger babies inside. And how much interference would the parents tolerate before abandoning their family? Larry had seen the baby stumble back into the tunnel, so we knew it was inside. We hoped it had made its way back to the nest chamber where I could reach it.

Carefully, I crept up the mound of sand above the nest chamber and took off the wooden cap that covered the pipe leading down to it. I slid my arm down the pipe until my fingers felt the warmth of little bodies. But which one was the injured owlet, if it was there at all? I pulled up one little ball of indignant fluff. Its eyes blinked furiously, but there was nothing wrong with its legs, which were kicking in all directions. Larry held that one while I tried again. This time I was lucky. The second ball of fluff had a leg that just flopped sideways in an alarming way. We popped the first baby back down the pipe, closed the cover and rushed into the house with our little cripple.

In our hospital room we x-rayed his leg and found he had broken it about an inch above his toes. We put a little cast on this leg from his toes to his knees. It was the finishing touch to the most ridiculous baby owl I've ever seen. His body was just a round ball of beige fluff with eyes on top and long legs sticking out below. He not only looked ridiculous, he sounded just as weird. The noise he made was somewhere between a buzz-saw and a rattle-snake, with a few frightened squeals added to the racket. We put him in a simulated nest under a dark towel warmed by a heat lamp. I stayed with him for a long time, making what I hoped were reassuring sounds while I stroked his little head. I fed him three times each day with tiny pieces of fresh mice, crickets and meal worms. It only took him about two days to learn that human sounds were good news, and he began to respond to us with excited chirps and wheezes.

When we had first seen his broken leg we knew we would have to keep him in the house for three weeks. We also knew he was at the critical age of focussing his vision and imprinting. But we couldn't have left him out in the cage with a broken leg; it wouldn't have healed by itself and would have made him unreleasable anyway. It was an easy decision to make. The little owl would live in the house with us. We hoped he would teach us something about family relationships in this species.

So this was how Cricket joined our family. Our first big problem was how to give him enough space, since Burrowing Owls spend a lot of time on or near open ground. Our second big problem was our two house cats. We were afraid that having a little owl running along on the floor would be just too tempting for the cats. How could we protect him from them?

We were really baffled until we began to think about how cats go hunting. First they try to sneak up on their prey and then, if the prey starts to run, they chase it. We knew that owls have better hearing than cats, but Cricket's best protection would be to make him unafraid of the cats so he wouldn't run from them. Then, we hoped, they would lose interest in him.

By the time Cricket had been in his cast for a week he had learned to stand on it and even walk a little. We brought him upstairs and put him on a big towel on the living room rug. The cats were fascinated. He looked so small and helpless, such an easy victim. They began to circle the towel, their tails twitching with anticipation. Finally the male cat, Dixon, crept towards Cricket. Cricket's eyes could focus well enough to see a blur coming his way, and to him that meant food. Screaming with delight, he stumbled forward towards the blur, flapping his little wings and opening his beak wide.

Dixon leapt backwards. This was not what he had in mind at all. Dixon hid under a chair to think his plan over a little more carefully. Our female cat, Moose, more timid by nature, escaped to the cats' nest and let Dixon handle the problem. She wasn't going near that thing, whatever it was. Meanwhile, Cricket stood at the edge of the towel, bewildered. Where had that nice blur and the hope of food gone? He started hobbling across the carpet, wheezing plaintively, and Dixon shot out from under the chair, up over the railing and joined Moose in the safety of the cats' nest. Since that first fateful day, Cricket and the cats have gone their separate ways, ignoring each other as much as possible.

It doesn't take long for a young owl's leg to heal, especially when it's being used, so we removed Cricket's cast in two weeks. That was some months ago, and today he is a very active member of the household. He has selected a corner behind a big chair as his "burrow." He gets to it through the narrow space between the chair and a copper wood bucket. He is a collector of oddments—key rings, erasers, bits of paper, pencil stubs and even

popsicle sticks. If anything small is missing, we look behind his chair. If Cricket is home, he screams in outrage at this violation of his privacy, lying on his back and kicking and having a real temper tantrum. If he is out when we raid his collection, we hear him muttering to himself when he returns and finds things not as they should be. We are sure this owl can count.

Cricket knows every nook and cranny of this house better than we do, and he is sometimes very hard to find. He loves to sit in the sun, and he follows it all around the east and south sides of the house. At night he perches on the lamps, and we have tried to control the mess by putting wicker placemats on top of all the shades. That way he gets the heat he loves, and we don't get the droppings down the shades. When visitors arrive, Cricket runs into his lair and waits until they are safely sitting down. Then he suddenly runs out on the carpet, and our visitors nearly have heart

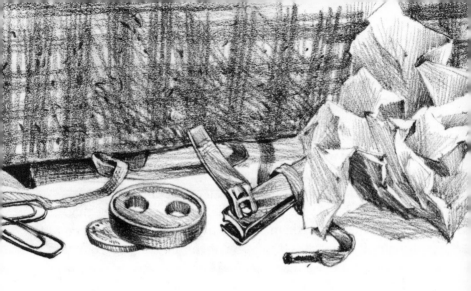

attacks if we've forgotten to warn them there's an owl around.

Granny is still outside for the summer and hasn't met Cricket yet. Whatever will she think of him? And what will Cricket think of her—a big black and yellow creature that can *fly*! Will his instincts tell him this is a big prairie hawk? Will he stay behind his chair for days? He has already met Sook, but Sook moves so fast that Cricket is still staring at the place where Sook was by the time Sook has been past it twice. Then we see Cricket watching the chandelier in a puzzled way and looking at us suspiciously, as if we were somehow responsible.

At bedtime, when Sook goes to his cage with his special mouse, Cricket also goes, voluntarily, to another big cage in our front hall. He is only there until morning, and we have built a little tunnel in this cage, so he can hide if he wants to. The only reason he goes to this cage voluntarily is the same reason that Sook does—for a nice fat mouse! Although the cats watch Sook hungrily and hopefully all night long, they never so much as glance at Cricket in his cage. They may even be thankful he's in the cage, that's the only time they can be sure where he is.

Over the few months that Cricket has lived in our midst, he has slowly but surely mastered our poor unwitting cats. At first he had just the one special chair, or "burrow," that he defended from them. Now he has taken over two other chairs. If he catches the cats on them snoozing peacefully, he flies at them screaming like a banshee while the cats scatter for cover, their tails twice normal size.

At night, when the lights go out, he starts stomping back and forth inside his cage, trying to see into the living room. At least once every night there is a squeal of rage and a stampede of cats, and then we know Cricket has spotted them fooling around with his treasures behind a chair. The cats never seem to learn that retribution comes with the dawn!

Chapter 11
GRANNY'S WINTER BABY

Each November, when Granny comes in for another winter, the big question on everyone's mind is what kind of owl baby will we get for her this year? Perhaps by now even Granny wonders about that. So far she has been a substitute mother to eleven baby Great Horned Owls, four baby Long-Eared Owls, two baby Screech Owls and now her latest baby, an infant Barn Owl. All her other foster babies have come from wild nests that have been damaged. But the baby Barn Owl's parents live right here. This is how it came to be Granny's latest baby.

For twelve years we have had a pair of injured Barn Owls living in one of our big compounds. Buster is almost twenty-five years old, with a beautiful snowy white face and breast and a caramel-coloured head and back. Bertha, his mate, is much younger, and her face and breast have a soft biege colour, instead of white. They both have heart-shaped faces and brown eyes. Like all Barn Owls, they are very good at producing babies when they have a protected nest and plenty of food.

Each year we let them have a spring brood and a late summer brood, and then we have to put a partition in their corridor and separate them from November until late March. Buster hates being kept away from Bertha, but it gives her a holiday from incubating eggs and brooding young and a chance to straighten out her legs and get some exercise.

All went well until this past January. I had heard some gleeful chippering calls from the Barn Owls for a few nights, but I didn't think much about it until I discovered too late that eager old Buster had dug himself a sneaky little tunnel under the partition that separated him from Bertha. When I saw him on her side of the barrier I feared the worst. Sure enough, there was the old devil grabbing a mouse from her food box, hotfooting it up to her nest and taking it inside. I followed him and heard the familiar sounds of housekeeping from the box. Then I broke the news to Larry.

We decided to take a ladder into the cage and see how far things had progressed. We might have guessed, knowing Buster, that even one day with Bertha would start the inevitable. Bertha had four new eggs under her, and she was spread over them like a blanket, hissing and screaming at us and trying to keep them warm. What on earth could we do? Because the weather was mild for January, we decided to chance leaving the eggs alone. After all, she had done the hard work in producing them, and if we took them away now she would only produce more. That would be harder on her than letting her incubate the ones she had.

Alas, a few days later the weather turned bitterly cold. We could picture poor Bertha out there in the big box, trying desperately to cover her eggs and getting colder and colder herself. The time to intervene had come. I put cotton wool in my pockets and went out to their cage with a ladder and a bag of pine needles. Buster screamed and Bertha hissed, but I took two of her eggs and put one in each pocket. Then I piled the pine needles into the box, making a hollow in the middle for the other two eggs. Bertha had left the box when I opened it, but she was soon back, scrambling over the pile of needles to get to her eggs. Meanwhile I scurried back to the warm house and went straight to Granny's cage with the precious eggs.

Poor Granny! She was sitting there contentedly on her annual egg, minding her own business, when all this happened. I think she can tell now when there is monkey business afoot, for she greeted me with a few uneasy croaks and looked suspiciously at my hands. Over the years so many babies have been slipped in under her and so many eggs have mysteriously vanished that she has learned to check out my hands first. Even so, she is such a pushover for a soft word and a caress that I can usually switch eggs under her tummy with one hand while I am grooming her with the other.

The only worrying thing now was the much smaller size of the Barn Owl eggs and the fact that there were two of them. Up until now, Granny has only coped with single eggs. For a day or so she seemed to be having a little trouble getting down low enough onto them. I even saw her stand up and peer between her feet in a special Granny way, looking puzzled, as if to say, "How many of these little things are there, anyway?"

Despite the oddities of size and number, Granny met the challenge and sat on patiently in her box, keeping her belly low and turning the strange little eggs at regular intervals. I hovered around, bringing her food and listening for any new sounds.

On the fourteenth day, I found her vibrating with excitement. Her feathers stood on end, and she began to croak in her agitated way. Between her croaks, as I stroked her, I was sure I could hear a funny sound. I looked quickly under her, but there were just the two eggs as usual. Then I heard it again—a very thin, high-pitched reedy sound—and it was definitely coming from her nest. This time Granny and I both looked under her. I picked up one egg and immediately heard it again. I could hardly believe it, but the sound was coming from the egg. Amazed, I looked closer. There seemed to be a little crack near one end. I put the egg hastily back under Granny. About an hour later the faint sound grew louder, and this time there was a hole in the egg. I could see something moving. Granny was beside herself with excitement at the prospect of another baby.

I hated to leave the cage to attend to other duties, but it was almost twelve hours before the tiny baby broke free of its egg and lay in Granny's soft nest. It was about the size of one of her toes. Granny was ecstatic and spent all her time nuzzling it, peeking at it through her feathers and generally welcoming it to the world. The baby was so small that I could hardly see it at first, but it was obviously getting plenty of attention. We were disappointed that the second egg never hatched— perhaps it had become too cold outside. The eggs left with Bertha outside didn't hatch either, although I'm sure she incubated them properly. But at least we had saved one. It was a lusty little owlet and could sit up, propped against Granny's leg, and bleat for food when it was only four days old.

No mere human could have given the owlet the perfect care it got from Granny. Every waking moment she groomed it, fed it, cleaned it or talked to it. She didn't seem to notice that it was too small to be hers, or that it was just about the homeliest baby in the world. She obviously thought it was perfection. We couldn't help but notice that she also kept it a lot cleaner than its parents had ever kept the babies in their own nest.

We also noticed that the baby was developing with the most amazing speed. Within a week it was about 10 cm/4 inches high and sitting up against Granny as if she were a mighty oak. In another week it was half as tall again and beginning to look around with a sort of half-lidded, drunken expression. By this time it was covered in thick white wool, except for its dark, bare face and lower legs. Baby Spectacled Owls are fuzzy white, with dark faces too, and we wondered if some special instinct stirred in Granny. Seeing her doting on this strange baby made me feel particularly sorry, knowing that the time for separation was coming.

During the baby's third week, two important things coincided. First, the weather turned very mild again, melting the snow and making it seem more like April than February. Secondly, the baby turned its head and really looked at me, weaving its body from side to side. There was no doubt that visual focus had started and we must get the owlet back to its parents. I watched Granny until she left the nest to bathe and preen, and then I gathered her up in my arms and took her upstairs, struggling and croaking in alarm. Then I rushed down to her nest, picked up the babe and carried it carefully out to its parents' nest. I climbed the ladder I had left in their cage and pushed the now screaming baby through the door of the nest box.

Talk about pandemonium! Buster and Bertha just erupted from the box and flew screeching around the cage, laying whitewash over everything, including me! The baby squawked and hissed from the box. I got out of the cage as fast as I could and waited for the din to subside. Pretty soon the mother flew up to the door and peered inside. The baby was so overwrought by all that had happened that it screamed anew and the mother nearly fell off her perch in shock. Whatever must she have thought at finding a big white baby inside? Slowly and carefully she went into the box. Like magic, the hissing and clicking changed to food-begging cries. I tossed two fresh mice onto the ground in plain view. Almost at the same moment I heard Bertha calling for food as well, and Buster came tearing down the corridor to his food box, saw the mice, grabbed one and hustled back. Soon he returned for the other, looking very important all of a sudden, now that he had such a big responsibility again.

A few days later, when I went back for the ladder, I couldn't resist taking a little peek. There was the baby,

pressed back against its natural mother, staring at the intruding human face with an expression of real horror. Its mother looked twice her normal size, every feather on end, hissing and swaying. It had all worked, after all, thanks to Granny and her tremendous instinct to be a loving mother.

Naturally, I had to console Granny for the disappearance of yet another baby, but she seems to be getting used to these vanishing acts. Eggs and babies appear from nowhere, are hers for a brief time and just as mysteriously disappear again. She is beginning to take it all in her stride, so long as I remain her mate and companion. This year there was only a lull of about four weeks between the Barn Owl episode and the arrival of the first foundling Great Horned owlet of the season. Granny hardly had time to get used to her evenings upstairs at my desk, watching the cats and Sook and the television before she was called back to the duties of motherhood again. What an incredible, wonderful creature she is. Whatever would we do without her?

Chapter 12
GRANNY'S GANG

This book has been all about putting owls to work to help other owls grow up and go free. No two years are the same because we never know what sort of owl will arrive next or when it will come. But we *do* know that babies from the wild must be with their own species once their eyes focus. If they aren't, they won't develop the right social image to live normally with their own kind when they have grown up.

How we handle the babies is all a matter of timing. Some years, the orphaned owlets are the same age as those in our nests here, and they can be put straight into these nests. Then Granny doesn't have much to do, and she can go outside earlier and watch the flowers opening.

Other years, the orphans are too young—sometimes just eggs—and then Granny really has her "hands" full.

Granny isn't the only foster parent we have. You've read about Pops and the Barn Owls and how they raise the owlets that Granny started on the right track. But what about some of the other kinds of owls? Over the years we have found other owl helpers for these different species. They are outside, waiting to take on Granny's "graduates" or to foster them from the beginning. You have met Tiglet, the bachelor Screech Owl, who hits people on the head. This year he surprised even himself by taking mice to six squeaking babies that suddenly

materialized in his cage. Sook, the little Saw-Whet Owl, and young Cricket, the Burrowing Owl, wait off stage for their chance to prove themselves members of the foster parents gang.

There are also several owls you haven't met, who live outside. There is a Long-Eared Owl called Ah-So. She doesn't have a mate, and one of her wings doesn't work properly, but she raised the four Long-Eared Owls that Granny fed first. And then there's Big Woo, a Great Grey Owl, who lays eggs hopefully each year. Last year she got a wild baby to raise that she thought was her very own. Two Barred Owls, Ajax and Andromeda, haven't made fertilized eggs yet either. But *they're* sure those little Barred Owlets that arrive so regularly must be their natural babies.

Also outside are the two little Saw-Whets, Samson and Delilah, who bring forth their own little beauties each year and would certainly feed any other squeakers they found sitting in their cage. Then there are our Snowy Owls, Ninotchka and Potchka, who, after six years of raising their own broods, got their very first orphan from the Arctic this past summer. And finally, our little Boreal Owls, Bertie and Tweet-Bird, after three years produced their first clutch of eggs and have a big, fat, smoke-grey baby to show for their

years of waiting. Now we are ready for orphaned baby
Boreal Owls from the wild too.

What will the next season bring? Large or small, new
babies will be all the same to Granny. Each one is treasured
as if it were her very own. I turn and look at her so fondly,
as she sits dozing behind my chair, gathering strength for
the coming season. Like a general with her army, her gang
is in place, waiting for the spring—for the new crop of
babies that will arrive with the tulips, smelling faintly of
woodland moss and sweet meadow grass.